Secretary's DESK GUIDE to Punctuation and Spelling, Word Division and Hyphenation

PRENTICE HALL
Englewood Cliffs, New Jersey 07632

Copyright MCMLV by

PRENTICE-HALL, INC.

Englewood Cliffs, New Jersey

ISBN 0-13-798463-4

PRINTED IN THE UNITED STATES OF AMERICA

CONTENTS

Ready Reference Material

1

Mechanical Techniques of Better Writing: Punctuation

FEW secretaries (or bosses either) are experts when it comes to the fine points of English language. Yet, as a secretary, you are expected to handle every type of written assignment quickly and flawlessly—and this means tackling a wide variety of English problems every working day.

That's why this unique Guide has been prepared especially for secretaries. It will help you whenever you have a problem in spelling, punctuation, word division or hyphenation. It will show you the correct way to handle complicated plurals, unusual possessives, peculiar hyphenations, and much more.

If you make a sincere effort to master and apply the principles in this Guide, you will find that it will not only upgrade your work, but save you considerable time and effort as well.

Punctuation

Punctuation marks. The chief marks of punctuation are listed below. Those with which the secretary is chiefly concerned are indicated by boldface type, and their most important uses are explained.

The chief marks of punctuation are:

´	Accent, acute	{ }	Brace
`	Accent, grave	[ ]	**Brackets**
'	**Apostrophe**	∧	Caret
*	**Asterisk**		

Mark		Name
¸	(ç)	Cedilla
^		Circumflex
:		**Colon**
,		**Comma**
†		Dagger
¨	(ö)	Dieresis
‡		Double dagger
* * * or . . .		Ellipsis
!		Exclamation point
-		**Hyphen**
. . .		Leaders
¶		Paragraph
‖		Parallels
( )		**Parentheses**
.		**Period**
?		**Question mark (Interrogation point)**
" "		**Quotation marks**
§		Section
;		**Semicolon**
~		Tilde
——		Underscore
/		Virgule

Apostrophe. *Possessives.* Use the apostrophe to indicate the possessive case of nouns. Do not use the apostrophe to indicate the possessive case of pronouns.

John's sons' its

Contractions. Use the apostrophe to denote a contraction or omission of letters. Place the apostrophe where the letter or letters are omitted.

it's for *it is* — *ass'n* for *association*
haven't for *have not* — class of '39

BUT omit the apostrophe in contractions formed by dropping the first letters of a word if the contraction has come into common usage.

phone plane

Letters and symbols. Use the apostrophe to form the plurals of letters and symbols.

p's and q's 5's #'s the 1920's

Words. Use an apostrophe to indicate the plural of a word referred to as a word, without regard to its meaning, but use the regularly formed plural if a meaning is attached to the word.

There are three *but's* in the sentence.
The *yeas* have it.
There are eight *threes* in twenty-four.

Abbreviations. Use an apostrophe to denote the plural or some other form of an abbreviation.

three O.K.'s O.K.'d V.I.P.'s

Asterisk. *Red figures.* An asterisk may be used in a financial statement to indicate a red figure, that is, a deficit, decrease, or loss. It is placed immediately *after* the figure.

Profit or Loss*
$18,538
682*

Reference. An asterisk may be used to denote a reference to a footnote. The asterisk *follows* the figure, but *precedes* the footnote.

Comma. *Apositives.* Use a comma to set off an apositive, that is, an expression that explains or gives additional information about a preceding expression.

The senior partner, *Mr. Edwards,* is in Europe.

BUT do not separate two nouns, one of which identifies the other.

The witness *Jones* testified about the capitalization of the company.

Cities and states. Separate the name of a city from the name of a state; also, separate the name of the state from the rest of the sentence.

Brown Company of Auburn, *New York,* has reduced turnover 50 per cent.

Compound predicates. Compound predicates are not usually separated by commas.

The total number of employees is increasing *and* will continue to increase for several more years.

Compound sentences. Separate the independent clauses of a compound sentence by a comma, unless the thoughts expressed require a more emphatic separation than the comma. The comma precedes the conjunction.

We appreciate very much your offer, *but* we are unable to accept it because of previous commitments.

The comma may be omitted before *and* if the clauses are short and closely connected in thought.

Schedules A-1 and A-2 were prepared today *and* the others will be prepared tomorrow.

Dash and comma. Do not use a dash and a comma together.

Dates. Separate the day of the month from the year by a comma. If no day is given, separate the month from the year by a comma. The trend is to omit the comma after the year, unless the construction of the sentence requires punctuation.

. . . payable March 12, 1950 to stockholders.
. . . as of March, 1950, the stockholders . . .

Ellipsis. Use a comma to indicate that one or more words, easily understood, have been omitted. (A construction of this type is known as an *ellipsis.*)

The employer contributed 60 per cent; the employees, 40 per cent.

Essential and nonessential phrases and clauses. A restrictive phrase or clause is one that is essential to the meaning of the sentence and is not merely descriptive or parenthetic; it should not be set off by commas. A nonrestrictive phrase or clause is one that adds an additional thought to the sentence but is not essential to the meaning of the sentence; it should be set off by commas.

The accountant *who testified in the case* is a close friend of the defendant.

The article, prepared by R. S. James, describes the utilization of a common design for three plants.

Introductory words. Use a comma to separate an introductory word from the rest of the sentence.

Yes, the meeting will be held as scheduled.

Inseparables. Do not place a comma between words that belong together and are interdependent, such as a verb and its subject or object or predicate nominative, or a limiting clause and its antecedent.

In the following examples the commas in brackets should be omitted.

The rapid advancement of the company to its present enviable position in the publishing world [,] is attributable largely to the acumen and energy of its founders. (The comma separates the subject "advancement" from its verb "is.")

The revision combines with the first edition's thoroughness [,] a constructive viewpoint, a wide range of practices, and up-to-date methods. (The comma separates the verb "combines" from its objects "viewpoint," "range," and "methods.")

The leeway allowed the defendants in this trial, as in all others [,] where justice prevails, is in sharp contrast to the treatment accorded defendants in totalitarian countries. (The "where" starts a limiting relative clause modifying "others.")

Names. Do not use a comma between a name and *of* indicating place or position.

Brown Company *of* Auburn, New York
Mr. Edwards *of* Robinson & Co.
Mr. Nash *of* counsel

Place a comma between a name and *Inc.*, *Sr.*, etc.

Lever Brothers, Ltd. Mr. R. G. Jones, Sr.

Numbers. Use a comma when writing figures in thousands, BUT NOT in house, room, post office box, and telephone numbers.

$15,800.65 3,800 1381 Vinton Avenue P. O. Box 4671 GR 5-4251

Parentheses and comma. Use a comma after a closing parenthesis if the construction of the sentence requires a comma. Never use a comma before a parenthesis or an expression enclosed in parentheses.

When packing the brief case, include pencils (preferably soft lead), erasers, and a seven-column analysis pad.

Parenthetical words and phrases. A comma precedes and follows parenthetical or defining words or phrases unless the connection is close and smooth enough not to call for a pause in reading.

Furthermore, credit obligations may be paid out of capital items.

If, *on the other hand,* the economic condition of the country improves . . .

He was *perhaps* busy at the time.

That equipment is expensive and *therefore* does not appeal to economy-minded firms.

BUT distinguish between words used parenthetically and the same words used as adverbs.

However, I shall follow your advice. (Parenthetical)

However early he arrives at his office, his secretary is always there before him. (Adverb)

Thus was a fortune built from nothing. (Adverb)

Thus, the assignment does not represent the substitution of one liability for another. (Parenthetical)

Participial phrases. Do not separate a participle from the noun it modifies when the noun is not the subject and the expression is not closely connected with the rest of the sentence. In transcribing, the natural tendency is to strike a comma where the virgule appears in the following sentence, necessitating an erasure.

The company's financial operations/ being controlled through budgets, additions to fixed assets are usually planned far in advance.

Phrases with a common element. Place a comma before a word or words that are common to two or more phrases but are expressed only after the last phrase. In the following examples the commas in brackets are frequently *omitted in error.*

The report was documented with references to many, if not all [,] of the recent tax·court decisions on the question. (The words "of the . . ." are common to "many" and to "all.")

The treasurer's reports are clearer, more concise, more accurate [,] than those of the advertising manager. (The words "than those . . ." are common to "clearer," "more concise," and "more accurate.")

NOTE: If the phrases are connected by a conjunction, the comma is not needed.

. . . are clearer, more concise, *and* more accurate than those . . .

Quotations. Set off direct quotations by commas.

His reply was, "I am not interested in the matter."

"I am not interested in the matter," he replied.

But if a question mark is needed at the end of the quotation, do not use a comma.

> "What is the lowest price you can quote?" he inquired.

Quotation marks and comma. Place the comma on the *inside* of quotation marks.

> When he spoke of "overtime," I thought he meant over forty hours.

Series. Separate three or more words and phrases in a series by a comma. Use the comma before the conjunction connecting the last two members of a series.

> Thus, we speak of buying goods on credit, of a merchant's credit, *and* of making a payment by credit.
>
> The business of the company is the wholesale distribution of silverware, watches, diamonds, *and* semiprecious stones.

But do not use a comma between two parallel constructions joined by a conjunction.

> This amount is equal to the covered loss less (1) the coinsurance deduction *and* (2) the normal loss.
>
> He can ask for changes in the estimate *or* for a completely revised estimate.

Colon. *Introduction to lists, tabulations.* The most frequent use of the colon is after a word, phrase, or sentence that introduces lists, a series, tabulations, extracts, texts, and explanations that are in apposition to the introductory words.

> The following is an extract from the report:
>
> These conditions must exist:

But do not use a colon to introduce a series of items that are the direct objects of a preposition or verb or that follow a form of the verb *to be.*

> Wrong: The requirements of a good secretary *are:* ability to take rapid dictation and to transcribe it rapidly; ability to spell correctly and to use the dictionary to the best advantage; familiarity with . . . (Omit the colon.)

Note: a colon may precede a formal tabulation even when the tabulated words or phrases are the objects of a preposition or verb or follow a form of the verb *to be.*

The requirements of a good secretary are:
Ability to take rapid dictation and to transcribe it rapidly
Ability to spell correctly and to use the dictionary to the best advantage
Familiarity with . . .

Time. Use a colon to indicate clock time, unless the time indicated is on the hour.

4 A.M. 9:30 P.M.

Dash and colon. Do not use a dash with a colon.

Dash. *Principal use.* The dash is used principally to set off explanatory clauses, to indicate abrupt changes in the continuity of expression, and to set off a thought that is repeated for emphasis.

Series. A dash may be used before or after a clause that summarizes a series of words or phrases, but a colon is more common *after* such a clause.

Wage and Hour, Arbitration, Union Contracts—these are only a few of the services in our Complete Labor Equipment.

Our Complete Labor Equipment includes six services: Wage and Hour, Employee Relations, Union Contracts, Labor Relations, State Labor Law, and Pension and Profit Sharing.

Compound name of accounts. Usually a hyphen is used to join the parts of a compound word, but in accounting a *dash* is used to join a *compound name* of an account.

Allowance for depreciation—office
Allowance for depreciation—plant

Dash and other punctuation marks. A dash may be used after an abbreviating period. If the material set off by dashes requires an interrogation or exclamation point, retain the punctuation before the second dash. Do not use a dash with a comma or semicolon. Do not use a dash and colon together before a list of items.

The check is now O.K.—he made a large deposit.

The head of the personnel department—is his name Donovan or O'Donovan?—said he thought there would be an opening next week.

Hyphens. *Division of words.* Use a hyphen at the end of a line to show that part of a word has been carried over to another line.

Compound terms. Use a hyphen as a connecting link in some compound terms.

Series of hyphenated words. In a series of hyphenated words having a common base, place a hyphen after the first element of each word and write the base after the last word only.

long- and short-term notes
a two-, three-, or four-year audit

Time. Use a hyphen to indicate a span of time.

The report covers the fiscal year 1981-82.

Parentheses and brackets. *Brackets.* If your typewriter has a bracket key, use brackets to enclose comments or explanations in quoted material, to rectify mistakes, and to enclose parentheses within parentheses; otherwise, use parentheses for these purposes. If necessary, brackets can be made by using the virgule and the dash.

Explanatory expressions. Use parentheses to enclose parenthetical or explanatory expressions that are outside the general structure of the sentence. Parentheses indicate a stronger separation than do commas or dashes.

The place at which an incorporators' meeting (sometimes called the first meeting of the stockholders) is to be held is usually determined by statute.

Figures. Enclose a figure in parentheses when it follows an amount that has been written out in words, and when the American equivalent of foreign currency is given.

The capitalization of the company is £100,000 ($280,000).
Seven thousand five hundred (7,500) dollars
Seven thousand five hundred dollars ($7,500)

NOTE: If the figure is written before the word "dollars," do not use the dollar sign; if the figure is written after the word "dollars," use the dollar sign. This rule also applies to the per cent sign.

Enumerations. Enclose in parentheses letters or numbers in enumerations run into the text.

The company's stock is divided into two kinds: (1) common stock and (2) preferred stock.

Red figures. Parentheses may be used in a column of figures to enclose a red figure, that is, a decrease, deficit, or loss. They are also frequently used to enclose a figure that is subtracted, rather than added.

Buildings, machinery, and equipment	$67,062,431
Less—Depreciation and amortization	(26,048,626)
	$41,013,805

NOTE: Zeroes should neither be placed in parentheses nor typed in red. Obviously, a zero cannot represent a deficit or loss, and it cannot be added or subtracted.

Single (closing) parentheses. Parentheses are usually used in pairs, but a single closing parenthesis may be used instead of a period to follow a letter or small roman numeral in outlines and in lettering and numbering paragraphs.

Periods. *Sentences.* Place a period at the end of a declarative or imperative sentence.

The contract was signed last week. (Declarative)
Hold the report until next month. (Imperative)

Enumerated lists. Omit the period after items in enumerated lists unless the items make complete sentences.

Initials and abbreviations. Place a period after initials and, usually, after abbreviations. Preferably, the periods are omitted between initials standing for federal agencies.

Ph.D. C.O.D. *ibid.* Chas. Thos. R. E. Smith CAA

Outlines. Place a period after each letter or number in an outline or itemized list unless the letter or number is enclosed in parentheses.

Omissions. Omit the period after:

Contractions (ass'n, sec'y)

Roman numerals, except in an outline (Schedule II, George V)

Sums of money in dollar denominations, unless cents are added ($50, $50.25)

Shortened forms of names and words in common use (Ed, Will, ad, memo, per cent, photo)

Letters identifying radio stations (WOR, NBC)

Periods and parentheses. When an expression in parentheses comes at the end of a sentence and is part of the sentence, put the period outside the parentheses; if the expression is independent of the sentence and a period is necessary, place the period within the parentheses.

The long term debt shows a decrease of $1,000,000 (see Note 1).

The Consolidated Balance Sheet shows accrued taxes of $703,-138.98. (This amount includes a deficiency assessment by the Treasury Department of $572,723.21.)

BUT do not use a period when a complete declarative or imperative sentence is enclosed in parentheses *within a sentence.*

The honorary chairman of the board (he retired from active duty several years ago) addressed the Quarter-Century Club.

Question mark (interrogation point). *Interrogative sentences.* Place a question mark after a direct question but not after an indirect question.

Have you heard the decision that was made at the conference? (Direct)
Mr. Rogers asked me, "When will the annual report be ready for the printer?" (Direct)
Mr. Rogers asked me when the annual report would be ready for the printer. (Indirect)

Requests. Do not place a question mark after a question that is a request to which no answer is expected.

Will you please return the signed copy as soon as possible.

Queries. A question mark enclosed in parentheses may be used to query the accuracy of a fact or figure. Other punctuation is not affected by this use of the question mark.

The contract was signed September 5 (?), 1945.

Series of questions. A question mark is usually placed after each question in a series included within one sentence, and each question usually begins with a capital.

What will be the effect of the devaluation of the pound if other countries devalue their currencies? If wages are not increased in proportion to the devaluation? If Britain does not develop her market in this country?

BUT the question mark may be omitted in a series of questions in a construction like the one in the following example.

Who is responsible for (a) typing the report, (b) footing the totals, (c) making the corrections?

Quotation Marks. *Direct quotations.* Enclose the exact words of a speaker or writer in quotation marks, but do not enclose words that are not quoted exactly. The quoted material may be a word or several paragraphs in length.

On the 15th he wrote, "Please consider the contract canceled if the goods are not shipped by the 10th of next month."

On the 15th he wrote that the company should consider the contract canceled if the goods were not shipped by the tenth of next month.

He wrote that he was "no longer interested" in the proposition.

BUT do not use quotation marks when the name of the speaker or writer immediately precedes the quoted material or in question and answer material.

Mr. Edwards: In my opinion the machine is worthless.
Mr. Roberts: Upon what do you base that opinion?

Paragraphs. When quoted material is more than one paragraph in length, place quotation marks at the beginning of each paragraph and at the close of the last paragraph.

Definitions. Use quotation marks to enclose a word or phrase that is accompanied by its definition.

The party against whom garnishment proceedings are brought is called the "garnishee."

"Bankruptcy insolvency" means that a debtor's total assets are less than his total liabilities.

Unusual words or trade terms. Use quotation marks to enclose an unusual word or phrase or one used with a special trade meaning the first time the term is used. It is not necessary to use the quotation marks when the term is repeated.

This "pyramiding" was carried to an extreme in the public utility field.

In "spot" markets, commodities are bought and sold in specific lots and grades with a definite delivery date specified.

Titles and names. Use quotation marks to enclose the titles of:

Articles
Books, chapters, or parts of books
Brochures, pamphlets
Operas
Paintings
Plays, motion pictures, sketches
Poems
Songs

NOTE: In letters or advertising material, the title of a book may be capitalized for emphasis. In printed material the title of a book is usually italicized; therefore, in preparing material for the printer, underline the title of a book.

BUT do not use quotation marks with:

Names of periodicals and well known publications, such as Who's Who and dictionaries

The Bible or names of its books or other parts of it

Movements of a symphony, concerto, or other compositions, or names of numbered compositions

Single quotation marks. Use single quotation marks to enclose a quotation within a quotation.

Last week he wrote, "It is understood that the report 'must be delivered on or before the 30th.' "

Placement of quotation marks. Always place a period or comma inside quotation marks.

The account was marked "paid," but he never received a receipt.
The check was marked "canceled."
Many thanks for sending me a copy of Dr. Jones' book, "The Trade of Nations."

Some secretaries question the practice of always placing the period and comma *inside* quotation marks, but this is the practice recommended by leading American authorities. The British set periods and commas outside quotation marks when they are not part of the quotation, just as we do with interrogation points and exclamation points, but American printers have never adopted this practice. Typed material customarily follows the printed style.

Always place colons and semicolons outside quotation marks.

> Turn to the chapter entitled "Consideration for Stock"; the reference is in the first paragraph.

Interrogation and exclamation points come before or after the quotation marks, depending upon the meaning of the text.

> Who is the author of "Miracle of the Bells" ? (The entire question is not quoted.)
>
> He shouted, "I will never consent to those terms!" (The exclamation is part of the quotation.)

Semicolon. *Compound sentences.* A semicolon may be used to separate the parts of a compound sentence when the comma and conjunction are omitted.

> The adjustment has been made; the file has been closed.

Long, involved clauses. Use a semicolon to separate long, involved clauses.

> A low rate of interest usually reflects easy conditions and a rather inactive industrial situation; a high rate indicates money stringency and industrial activity.

Punctuated clauses. Use a semicolon to separate clauses that are punctuated by commas.

> On the other hand, if the turnover is low in comparison with the normal figure, it shows just the opposite; that is, weaker sales policy, and poorer purchasing ability and stock control than the average.

Series. In enumerations use semicolons to separate the items unless they are short and simple; also, to separate items that contain commas.

> The three classes of long bills are (1) bills drawn in ordinary business operations; (2) long bills arising from the making of foreign loans; (3) finance bills.
>
> The most important of these services are published by Moody's Investors Service, Inc.; Standard & Poor's Corporation; and Fitch Publishing Co., Inc.

Before a conjunctive adverb. Use a semicolon before an adverb that serves the purpose of a conjunction. The conjunctive adverbs are *accordingly, also, beside, consequently, furthermore, hence, however, indeed, likewise, moreover, nevertheless, otherwise, similarly, so, still, therefore, thus.*

> He telephoned that he did not plan to leave until next week; *therefore,* I did not consider it necessary to send the report to him by airmail.

Quotation marks and semicolon. Place the semicolon *outside* quotation marks.

Parentheses and semicolon. Use a semicolon after a closing parenthesis if the construction of the sentence requires a semicolon. Never use a comma or semicolon before a parenthesis or an expression enclosed in parentheses.

2

Mechanical Techniques of Better Writing: Spelling, Division, and Hyphenation of Words

Spelling

Plurals. *Words ending in o.* All words ending in *o* preceded by a vowel form the plural by adding *s*, as in *folios, trios, studios.* Generally, words ending in *o* preceded by a consonant form the plural by adding *es*, as in *Negroes, potatoes, heroes;* a few form the plural by adding *s*, as in *solos, dynamos.* Some have both forms as in *cargoes* or *cargos, mottoes* or *mottos.*

Words ending in y. Words ending in *y* preceded by a vowel form the plural by adding *s*—for example, *attorneys, days;* BUT words ending in *y* preceded by a consonant change the *y* to *i* and add *es, as in ladies, berries, countries, counties.*

Abbreviations. The plural of abbreviations, figures, and the like is formed by the use of the apostrophe and an *s*, as in *p's and q's, size 6's, Ph.D.'s.*

Combinations of i and e. Learn the following rhyme and you are not likely to make a mistake in combining *i* and *e*.

> The *i* before *e*
> Except after *c*,
> Or when sounded like *a*
> As in *neighbor* and *weigh.*

EXCEPTIONS: either, neither, seize, weir, weird, sheik, leisure, inveigle, plebeian, financier, specie, conscience.

Doubling the consonant. *One-syllable words.* Double the final consonant of a one-syllable word before adding a suffix beginning with a vowel, if the final consonant is preceded by a single vowel.

run, running   pin, pinning   plot, plotted   bag, baggage

BUT, if the final consonant is preceded by another consonant or by two vowels, do not double the final consonant.

brief, briefer   look, looked   act, acting   laud, laudable

Words of more than one syllable. Double the final consonant of a word of more than one syllable before adding a suffix beginning with a vowel if the final consonant is preceded by a vowel and the word is accented on the last syllable.

begin, beginning   transfer, transferring

BUT when the accent does not fall on the last syllable or the final consonant is preceded by another consonant, do not double the final consonant.

profit, profited   desert, deserting   travel, traveler   cancel, canceling

Words ending in silent e. *Suffixes beginning with a vowel.* Words ending in a silent *e* generally drop the *e* before a suffix beginning with a vowel. See also SUFFIXES: –ABLE, –OUS.

bride, bridal	argue, arguable
guide, guidance	owe, owing
ice, icing	judge, judging
use, usable, using	sale, salable (*variant*, saleable)

EXCEPTIONS:

dye	hoe	tinge
eye	shoe	toe
hie	singe	vie

Suffixes beginning with a consonant. Words ending in silent *e* generally retain the *e* before suffixes beginning with a consonant, unless another vowel precedes the final *e*.

pale, paleness	excite, excitement	due, duly
hate, hateful	argue, argument	

EXCEPTIONS:

abridgment	nursling
acknowledgment	wholly
judgment	

Words ending in ie. Words ending in *ie* drop the *e* and change the *i* to *y* before adding the *ing*.

die, dying	lie, lying

Suffixes: –able, –ous. Words ending in *e* preceded by *c* or *g* do not drop the final *e* before the suffixes –able or –ous, but do drop the final *e* before the suffix –ible.

service, serviceable	manage, manageable
courage, courageous	advantage, advantageous
deduce, deducible	convince, convincible

The –able, –ible difficulty. If a word has an *–ation* form, it always takes the suffix *–able* instead of *–ible*. Thus, *application, applicable; reparation, reparable.* However, many words that do not have an *–ation* form also take the suffix *–able,* which is far more common than the suffix *–ible.* There is no rule distinguishing the groups.

Suffixes: –ance or –ence. When the suffix is preceded by *c* having the sound of *k*, or *g* having a hard sound, use *ance, ancy,* or *ant;* when *c* has the sound of *s*, or *g* the sound of *j*, use *ence, ency*, or *ent.*

convalescence	indigent
significant	extravagant
negligence	

If the suffix is preceded by a letter other than *c* or *g* and you are in doubt about the spelling, consult the dictionary.

Suffixes: –ise or –ize. There is no rule governing the use of *–ise* or *–ize.* The words in the following list, and their derivatives and compounds, are spelled with *–ise.* The preferable American spelling for all other words is *–ize.*

advertise	excise
advise	exercise
apprise	exorcise
arise	franchise
chastise	improvise
circumcise	incise
comprise	merchandise
compromise	premise
demise	reprise
despise	revise
devise	supervise
disguise	surmise
enterprise	surprise

Words ending in c. When a word ends in *c*, insert a *k* before adding a suffix beginning with *e*, *i*, or *y*.

picnic, picnicking, picnicked
traffic, trafficker, trafficking

Words ending in –sede, –ceed, or –cede. Only one word in our language ends in *–sede: supersede.* Only three end in *–ceed: proceed, exceed, succeed.* All the others end in *–cede.* Remember, also, that *proceed* changes its form in *procedure.*

Words ending in y preceded by a consonant. Words ending in *y* preceded by a consonant generally change the *y* to *i* before any suffix except one beginning with *i*.

modify, modifying, modifier, modification
lonely, lonelier, loneliness
worry, worrisome, worried

EXCEPTIONS: 1. Adjectives of one syllable have two forms in the comparative and superlative.

dry	drier, driest or dryer, dryest	shy	shier, shiest or shyer, shyest	spry	sprier, spriest or spryer, spryest

2. Adjectives of one syllable usually retain the *y* before *ly* and *ness*.

shyly, shyness
dryly, dryness
spryly, spryness

3. The *y* is retained in compounds of *–ship* and *–like* and in derivatives of *lady* and *baby*.

secretaryship   ladylike   ladyfinger   babyhood

The prefix dis–. Words formed by adding the prefix *dis–* are frequently misspelled because of doubt about whether the combined form has one *s* or two. The prefix is *dis–*. If the word to which the prefix is added begins with *s*, the combined form has two *s*'s; otherwise, the combined form has only one *s*.

dis–	appoint	disappoint
dis–	appear	disappear
dis–	satisfy	dissatisfy

Division of Words

Division of words at the end of a line. To avoid a ragged right-hand margin, it is sometimes essential to divide a word at the end of a line, but divide *only* when necessary. Try not to have two successive lines with a divided word at the end, and never have more than two. Avoid dividing the last word in a paragraph. Never divide the last word on a page, except in some legal documents where the last word is divided to show continuity.

The correct division of a word depends first of all on the breakdown of the word into syllables. The American dictionaries syllabicate according to pronunciation, and not according to derivation. If you do not know the proper division into syllables for a word, look up the word in the dictionary. There are, however, a few simple rules in addition to the rule of syllables that govern the division of a word.

Rules for the division of words at the end of a line.

1. Never divide words pronounced as one syllable.

through drowned gained

2. Never divide a four-letter word.

only into

3. Never separate one-letter syllables at the beginning of a word from the rest of the word.

around alone

4. Divide a word with a one-letter syllable within the word after the one-letter syllable, except in the case of the suffixes –able or –ible.

busi-ness sepa-rate medi-cal con-sider-able reduc-ible

NOTE: There are many words ending in *–able* or *–ible* in which the *a* or *i* does not form a syllable by itself. These words are divided after the *a* or *i*.

pos-si-ble chari-ta-ble ca-pa-ble

5. Do not carry over a two-letter syllable at the end of a word.

caller ex-pertly overly pur-chaser

6. Avoid separating two-letter syllables at the beginning of a word from the rest of the word.

eli-gi-ble   begin-ning   atten-tion   redeemed
(But re-deemed is preferable to redeem-ed.)

7. When the final consonant in a word is doubled before a suffix, the second consonant belongs with the letters following it.

run-ning   occur-ring

8. Do not carry over to the next line single or double consonants in the root word.

call-ing   forc-ing   divid-ing   fore-stall-ing

9. When two consonants occur within a word, divide the word between the consonants.

gram-mar   expres-sive   moun-tain   foun-da-tion

10. The following suffixes are not divisible:

–cial	–sion	–ceous
–sial	–tion	–tious
–tial	–gion	–geous
–cion	–cious	–gious

11. Avoid dividing a compound hyphenated word except where the hyphen naturally falls.

father-in-law   self-applause

12. Do not divide abbreviations.

Ph.D.   Y.W.C.A.   C.O.D.

13. Avoid dividing numbers. If it is necessary to divide, divide on a comma and retain the comma.

$1,548,-345,000

14. Divide dates between the day and the year, not between the month and the days.

. . . . .September 19,
1955 . . . .

15. Do not separate the initials of a name and avoid separating initials, titles, or degrees from the name; also avoid dividing proper names.

16. A dieresis is placed over a vowel to indicate its pronunciation as a separate syllable from the preceding vowel, as in coöper-

ate, reëntry. If the word is divided between these vowels, no dieresis is needed.

Compound Terms

Suggestions for forming compound terms. A compound term consists of two or more words written together as one word, or joined by a hyphen, or written separately but expressing a single idea. Thus *editor-in-chief, businessman,* and *attorney general* are all compounds. The authorities differ as to whether certain compounds should be written separately, hyphenated, or written as one word. When there is a choice, decide which form you prefer and follow the form you choose consistently. Of course, if your company has a style manual, you should follow it.

The following suggestions are a guide to forming compounds.

Adjectives. Hyphenate two or more words used as an adjective, such as *short-term* loan, *no-par* stock, *above-mentioned* law. Do not hyphenate color variations used as an adjective, such as *navy blue* dress, *light gray* paint.

Adverbs. Do not use a hyphen to connect an adverb and an adjective. Adverbs properly modify adjectives. Do not use a hyphen to connect an adverb ending in –ly and a past participle in such phrases as *efficiently managed firm, neatly typed report.*

Fractions. Hyphenate fractions when the numerator and the denominator are both one-word forms, such as *one-third, three-fourths, one-hundredth.*

Nationalities. Hyphenate two or more words to indicate that the person or thing shares in the qualities of both, as *Anglo-American, Sino-Japanese, Latin-American* (but not Latin America), *Scotch-Irish.*

Coined phrases. Hyphenate coined phrases, such as *middle-of-the-road course, pay-as-you-go, drive-it-yourself, ready-to-wear.*

Titles. Do not hyphenate titles such as *vice president, rear admiral, Chief of Staff,* but do hyphenate *secretary-treasurer* and other coined compounds. Also hyphenate *ex-President, President-elect,* and *vice-president-elect* (even though *vice president* alone is not hyphenated).

Prefixes. Compounds formed with the prefixes *inter–, non–, semi–,* and *sub–* are not hyphenated unless used with a proper noun—for example, *non-American.* Compounds formed with the prefix *self–* are hyphenated.

Approved forms of compounds. The following list indicates the preferred form for writing certain compounds that will recur in your work.

above-mentioned (adj.)
above-named (adj.)
aforesaid
afore-mentioned (adj.)
antitrust
bathhouse
bondholder
bookstore
breakdown (noun or adj.)
breakeven (adj.)
bylaws
by-product
car fare
carry-back
carry-forward
cashbook
change-over (noun)
charge-off (noun)
checkoff (noun)
close-out (noun or adj.)
copyright
cross-check (verb)
cross-refer (verb)
cross reference (noun)
first-class
first-hand
follow-up (noun or adj.)
good will
home office
inasmuch as
insofar as
intercompany
interoffice
interstate
lawsuit
leasehold
letterhead
livestock
long-term (adj.)
man power
make-up (noun)
newsstand
nonoperating
nonpayment
nonproductive
nonrecurring
nontaxable
no-par stock
offset
one-half (adj.)
one half of
overabsorbed
over-all (adj.)
overall (noun)
overpayment
overstatement
paid-in surplus
passbook
past-due (adj.)
pay day
payroll (noun or adjective)
per cent
postdated
post office (noun)
post-office (adj.)
post-war
pro forma
pro rata (adv.)
prorata (adj.)
prorate (verb)
right of way
safekeeping
second-class
secondhand
self-explanatory
semiannual
setup (noun)

set up (verb)
short-term (adj.)
shutdown (noun)
so-called
split-up (noun)
stockholder
storehouse
storeroom
straight-line (adj.)
sublease
subtreasury
tax-free (adj.)
taxwise
test check (noun)

Plurals of compound terms. In forming the plural of compound terms one word of which is a noun, the most important word takes the plural form.

aides-de-camp
adjutants general
ambassadors at large
assistant *attorneys* general
attorneys general
bills of lading
brigadier *generals*
brothers-in-law
controllers general
deputy *chiefs* of staff
general *counsels*
governors general
judge *advocates*
lieutenant *colonels*
maid *servants*
notaries public
presidents-elect
rights of way
sergeants at arms
sergeants major
surgeons general
trade *unions*
vice *chairmen*

When both words are of equal importance, both words take the plural form.

coats of *arms* *men employees*

When no word is of importance in itself, the last word takes the plural form.

follow-*ups*
forget-me-*nots*
jack-in-the-*pulpits*
pick-me-*ups*

When a noun is compounded and hyphenated with a preposition, the noun takes the plural form.

by-*products, hangers*-on, *listeners*-in, *passers*-by

When neither word in the compound term is a noun, the last word takes the plural form.

write-*offs,* charge-*offs,* split-*ups*

Compound nouns written as one word form their plurals regularly. Words ending in *–ful* are the only ones that cause any trouble.

cupfuls, tablespoonfuls, bucketfuls

When it is necessary to convey the meaning that more than one container was used, write the compound as two words and add *s* to the noun.

5 *cups* full, 2 *tablespoons* full, 4 *buckets* full

Possessives

Possessives are regularly formed by adding an apostrophe and *s* to the word, but there are exceptions.

Awkward or sibilant sounds. Drop the *s* and add only an apostrophe to form the possessive when the use of *'s* would cause a hissing or an awkward sound.

Moses' rod　　*Kansas'* son　　*executrix'* power
for *conscience'* sake　　for *appearance'* sake
for *goodness'* sake　　for *convenience'* sake

Words ending in s. The singular possessive of words ending in *s* is formed by adding *'s;* the plural possessive by adding only the apostrophe. Formerly, the accepted form for singular as well as plural nouns was the addition of an apostrophe without the *s*. The Government style manual still uses that form, but other authorities prefer the *'s* in almost all cases.

Controllers' duties　　Misses *Smiths'* reception
Mr. *Jones's* car　　*James's* position
the *Joneses'* car　　*bus's* motor

The use of the apostrophe without the *s* still prevails in poetic or biblical expressions.

Jesus' life, *Achilles'* heel, *Mars'* Hill

Words ending in ss. If a word ends in *ss*, form the possessive by adding an apostrophe without the *s*.

the *witness'* testimony
the *princess'* wedding
Strauss' waltzes

Of phrase. An *of* phrase may be used to show possession. When the thing possessed is a specific number or group belonging to the possessor, the *'s* also is used, thus forming a double possessive.

In his book he tried to imitate a novel *of* James *Street's*.
That remark *of* the *commentator's* aroused. . . . (A specific remark.)
Those investments *of* his *father's* are. . . . (Specific investments.)

When the thing possessed is not restricted or limited to a specific number or group, the *'s* is not used.

In his book he tried to imitate the novels *of* James *Street.*
The remarks *of* the *commentator* aroused. . . . (Generally speaking.)
The investments *of* his *father* are. . . . (Generally speaking.)

Appositives and explanatory words. Whenever possible, avoid the use of appositives or explanatory words with the possessive case. If the object possessed is named, the word nearest the object takes the possessive. If the object is not named and the appositive or explanatory words end the sentence, the first noun takes the possessive form. When in doubt, change the construction of the sentence and use the *of* phrase.

RIGHT: His guardian, *Mr. Nelson's,* control of the money. . . .
BETTER: Control of the money *by his guardian, Mr. Nelson.* . . .
RIGHT: The reception was held at her *aunt's,* Mrs. Mason.
RIGHT: In his writings, he tries to imitate his father, *James Street's,* novels.
BETTER: In his writings, he tries to imitate the novels *of his father,* James Street.

When the appositive is restrictive and, therefore, not set off by commas, the awkward construction does not arise.

The defendant *Adams's* defense

When the explanatory words are parenthetical, and especially when they are enclosed in parentheses, the construction *must* be changed to avoid the possessive.

AWKWARD: *Mrs. Ball's* (formerly Miss Brown) estate is. . . .
AWKWARD: Mrs. Ball, formerly *Miss Brown's,* estate is. . . .
AWKWARD: *Mrs. Ball's,* formerly *Miss Brown's,* estate is. . . .
BETTER: The estate *of Mrs. Ball,* formerly Miss Brown, is. . . .

Inanimate objects. An inanimate object cannot actually possess anything. It is usually better to show relation by the use of the *of* phrase. However, usage has attributed possession to some inanimate objects, especially those expressing time or measure.

one day's vacation
two weeks' pay
one additional day's pay
five dollars' worth
a month's delay
three months' delay
six pounds' weight

The italicized expressions are plural. Notice that the apostrophe *follows* the *s* instead of preceding it. Many of these expressions form compound adjectives and can be hyphenated instead of written as possessives.

a one-day vacation
a three-month delay
a six-pound weight
a three-ounce bottle

Possessive of compound nouns. The *singular* possessive of compound nouns is formed by adding *'s* to the word nearest the object possessed.

Attorney *general's* argument
John Brown, *Jr.'s* office
Mr. Mason of *Consolidated's* staff
notary *public's* seal
aide-de-*camp's* promotion

Use the *of* phrase to form the *plural* possessive of a compound noun.

arguments *of* the attorneys general
seals *of* notaries public
promotions *of* aides-de-camp